POEMS 1998-2016

POEMS 1998-2016

SEAN ELLIOTT

introduced by B.J. Sokol

Greenwich Exchange
London

Greenwich Exchange, London

First published in Great Britain in 2020
All rights reserved

Poems 1998-2016 © the estate of Sean Elliott, 2020

Printed and bound by imprintdigital.com
Cover design by December Publications
Tel: 07951511275

Greenwich Exchange website: www.greenex.co.uk

Cataloguing in Publication Data is available from the British Library

Cover art: courtesy of Shutterstock

Author Photo © Ginny Garramone

ISBN: 978-1-910996-35-5

CONTENTS

Sean Elliott: The Poet and the Poetry

Sean Elliott's verse is very special, as was the poet and man himself. This collection will allow the former, at least, to live on.

Reading this collection of Sean's lyrics may yield up a partial sense of the man who died so tragically young. However, Sean's kind of lyric poetry, which is the best kind, is not merely autobiographical or 'confessional'. He displayed no romantic fervor simply to 'celebrate myself ... sing myself', as Walt Whitman put it, and never betrayed tendencies to 'loafe at my ease', as Walt next had it. On the contrary – whether obliquely or directly, wittily or strenuously – Sean's questing poetry continually questions and re-questions all that it so vividly portrays as felt, seen or believed.

As a result, Sean's many precisely calibrated expressions of joy, sorrow, appreciation, confusion, and even (rarely) outrage all forge links with universal themes, and especially with the unending wonderment of being human.

For me, the beginning was when Sean came to London University fresh from Oxford in order to write a Ph.D. thesis under my 'supervision'. That was a bit rich, as never before had I had so small a demand made on me in order to guide a student, and also never before had I learned so much from any single student. Sean indeed had the rarest of gifts. One was his ability to hit the literary-critical nail immediately and squarely on the head – so that he proceeded directly not just to possible answers, but even more uncannily to the crucial critical questions posed by complex texts. His responses were balanced and immaculately expressed, and put into order impeccably. Therefore he was able to produce his thesis with freakishly few (actually no) errors or blemishes. His thinking and his prose were both so close to perfection that something that was in my experience wholly unprecedented occurred – the committee examining Sean's Ph.D. thesis recommended not even one single tiny alteration or improvement, but rather directly conferred a doctorate on him with only high praise.

Sean then developed into a talented critical writer, university lecturer and seminar leader, and became a colleague and friend. I soon learned that he was a poet as well, or rather a poet primarily.

Sean's poems notably speak for themselves, but I can add a few comments. They are, as a glance will show, transparently readable, requiring no intellectual or emotional gymnastics for comprehension. Thus these unclouded poems are highly 'accessible', as they say. However, here straightforward trajectories and unobtrusive imagery and diction coincide with hidden depths. I think I may have some clues as to how that comes about.

Despite his brilliance, Sean's personal demeanour reflected no egotistical tendencies at all – in that he was almost a walking oxymoron. His poetry is similar. Its rare quality arises in part from being absolutely and sometimes even brutally honest. Thus it displays alongside exceptional talents for perception and expression extraordinary bravery and truthfulness. Even when very painful topics are on view, such truthfulness makes these poems, paradoxically, delightful in the encounter.

Sean's poems thus display deep sorrows shorn of bitterness, joys celebrated without crowing, ironies exposed without sarcasm, due satire delivered without malice – and with all those the wit and polish of technical mastery. This takes me to a last point. Sean's poems repeatedly display the sonnet forms, the sestina forms, the inner rhymes and para-rhyms, the enjambment and other subtleties of scansion and rhythm that he explained to his creative writing classes. (In his stunning sonnet 'Hijacking the Poetry Class' his students include perennial 'Grumpy' and 'the Sweet Girl'.) But Sean uses formality not just as a technical trick, for he stands among those poets, the Elizabethans, Marvell and Yeats, for whom limiting form is actually liberating. Thus Sean speculates in his poem 'Wedding Ring' that 'Perhaps all art is in the limitations / we set ourselves' – although he also says in a poem about his father's mundane but joyous occupation 'All art is praise'.

Let me end with one example. The very title of Sean's sonnet 'Goat Song' contains an arcane pun, for the Greek word 'tragodia' literally means 'a goat song'. But one need not know about the etymology of 'tragedy' – which perhaps links drama with the cult of Dionysus – to be made sharply aware that in this poem Sean meditates on connections between eroticism and death. The body of the poem is by turns tender and ruefully ironic. Its contrasting final couplet, however, is rounded by an explicit pun that anyone will recognize. It states that his fatal illness provides: 'quite a footnote on the verb "to screw"'. Not that vulgarity is at all common in these poems, but neither is it, or any aspect of our mixed-skein lives, shunned or excluded.

B.J. Sokol
July 2019

THE STATUS OF THE CAT (2013)

DAWLISH

1) Back to Dawlish

I name the stragglers stranded at low-tide:
anemone, dog-whelk and hermit crab
shrink from my hand at large in their stone crib,
resilient and frail they flinch or hide.

I occupy my time with tiny things,
loafing about the beach and skimming stones
until, in rain, a glimpse of sunlight stuns
my mind, while cormorants stretch their drying wings.

Those passing clouds and sudden shafts of light
persuade the eye and almost move the heart,
as if this random world could lessen hurt
with something simple like a gull in flight

or somewhere silent like this seaside town
long after summer's fetes and fairs have gone.
The children hunched in school, the work begun,
the squares near empty where the litter's blown,

the hotels and amusements closed til spring,
small shops, old women in their heavy coats –
my lips read off my town like a list of notes
but miss a detail, some forgotten thing

inconsequential as the winter foam
stretching across the beach on a rising tide,

an absent word, unsaid but still implied,
like someone's voice, a sound to call me home.

2) Dawlish in April

Frail women in wheelchairs, worn faces tense
against the breeze, (their carers smoking in
a separate huddle) watch the glittering sea
with some distrust: its promises are vague,
its taxes dear and freighted with much loss.

3) Birthday Party

White steps uneven to prevent escapes
(age stumbles on irregularity),
the nurses breezy with efficiency,
extracting dotards from their daily scrapes;

we saw him shrunken in his easy chair,
no recognition for my mother's sake
when she unpacked his modest birthday cake.
We sang, my father waited by the car

too scared to join us, with his pipe
warming his hand against the Cornish chill.
We left the cake for grandad, one look back,

my teary mother gave her face a wipe
and off we drove. I counted stars, kept still,
and watched the fenceless hillsides turning black.

4) A Dare

The right day, coming home from school
along the beach, a sudden wave
would surge across the level sand,
four yards or more to strike the wall –
our game was only for the brave:
a well-timed sprint across the strand

meant dryness when you reached the stone
stairs to the town; to get it wrong
ensured a drenching and the pull
of thigh-high water; you were thrown
off balance, then you squelched along
the cold street home a dripping fool.

Today and inland. I avoid
such dares, dislike the blinding thrash
and scramble back to safety. Pride
too makes me cautious. Chance destroyed
my home one time. I save my cash,
walk slow, respect the waiting tide.

5) Lea Mount

The fir tree frozen by the early sun,
the iron fence above the chewed-up cliff
where I, school-blazored, stood that dawn
and watched her swim, already further off
than any friend of ours had ever gone.

I saw her heading out, too far from me,
towards the last trace of a fading moon,
the tide so high the submerged rocks were sheathed,
her costume bluer than the morning, soon
hard to distinguish from the April sea.

6) The Football Stand

'What if I am?' The numbness round my lips,
her voice now timorous, the football pitch
beyond the varnished benches trampled mud;

ridiculous, our dreams now in eclipse,
college and career lost in one quick switch,
I held her hand, felt drained of breath and blood.

A false alarm: not that I guessed it when
we sheltered there for three hours after school,
then nowhere for us but our parents and

the gossip of their working days. What men
have loved her since and was I just a fool,
planning our future on that rain-drenched stand?

7) Home in March
(during Foot and Mouth)

The wind was strong against us as we took
the track along the beach, my brother off
from work, myself back home regaining strength
after a fever and a smoker's cough
had sapped me for a month and everywhere
the sullen rumours and the empty stalls.
'Avoid the lanes and owners keep your dog
leashed at all times.' We stumble through the rules.
The countryside becomes a wreath of smoke,
a darker grey against the falling snow,
the silent farms, behind their makeshift signs
forbidding entry, hold no comfort now
and where I used to walk my girlfriend home
(along a half-swamped lane to sit beside
a shelf that held two books: *The Pilgrim's Progress*,
Paradise Lost), crossed strands of plastic hide
the curving path. I think of that stark room
washed in perpetual Sunday tedium,
the mug of tea, the reverential hush,
one bleached carnation on its fragile stem
and next to her warmth and closeness, lost to time.
My brother makes a joke, I turn to smile
and spot the oystercatchers on the beach,
searching the shoreline, mile on famished mile.

8) A Christmas Visit

'They know me here,' but how does that explain
these bundled old men by a disused bay,
their same few names, the farms of flint and clay,
the rain-damp laughter in a snaking lane?

Instead I let them baffle you with words:
that sandstone accent gentle on the tongue,
bald heads in pubs, the flushed, soft-spoken young
courting along the beach like winter birds.

You catch in the circuit of a smarting eye
two furrowed cliffs, dull red and massed above
the teenage couples warm in huddled love,
a half moon shredded by a changing sky.

We are two children recently dismissed:
my parents, clumsy as a stifled cough,
still miss my wife but will not tell me off
or stomach you. Abashed I touch your wrist

and by the locked theatre with its range
of green and scarlet lights I point to where
the moon-faced barometer chills the air –
one broken arm forever fixed on 'Change'.

9) The Farm

No comfort but in words; I hear the tread
of those I love and hide from; let me hold

this sorrow back. They'll say he never said
a word; they'll say he was a little cold.
That's what they'll say. No comfort but in words.
The muteness of the farm surrounds us and
no car will take this road. I watch the night,
my stomach burning with a loneliness
like Scotch and I will claim that I could stand
those late and childless hours: it was all right
once you had learned the knack. The branches press
against our house. No comfort but in words.

MY PARENTS

1) Morning on the Coast

So cold it holds the heart, the light of dawn
silvers the curtains and stirs an early gull;
my mother's shout and bacon on the grill
bully my sleep until I stumble down

the hard and cat-strewn stairs towards the day.
Edging behind their chairs, I quietly take
my disused place and watch my parents talk –
both sure of what the other needs to say.

Full of their coffee, with my breath a ghost,
I trudge the wreckage of abandoned shells
and skirt the torpid sea (the steaming hills
shimmer with newness in the clammy mist)

knowing that on the train their smiling son
will wonder how he can again discard
this stooped, unworldly couple on the coast –
while through the glass they wave, almost as one.

2) Saloons and Tomahawks

'Tell me a story, Dad, a sci-fi one!'
and you, 'There were these cowboys on the moon...'
Lover of westerns, *Shane*, *Stagecoach*, *High Noon*,
your bedtime stories finally came down
to saloons and tomahawks. The fastest gun,

once eyeing neighbours with a deadly sneer,
you wished to rustle steers for your career:
'There's not much call for that in Edgware, son.'

Ten years rode by, your *Star Trek*-gazing child
baffled you: after work you'd sketch away:
stern Indians, bent cactus trees, the wild
horses and charcoaled ranchers, while the shame
of being poor bruised you. Your hand would sway,
across the moon the whooping cowboys came.

3) Butchery

All art is praise and I would praise your knives
cleaving the frozen rabbit or the side
of beef you carried from the truck with pride
in your old strength. The curvy, laughing wives

would gather round you only, wanting Les
to serve them, pouting up towards your beard
of smiles. They pointed at the trays, you neared
and asked them what their husbands liked: 'O bless!

I wouldn't like to say!' More laughter and
discussions of the virtues of the meat
bundled in packets for their men to eat
in homely silence, while your fresh-scrubbed hand

still hovered in each woman's chambered mind.
You worked for little pay, came home to us,
your wife and children and the usual fuss,
bearing your steak and desperate to unwind.

Older and half-retired, beyond the bleed
and dribble of the butcher's shop, you trail
behind my mother now; do calls assail
you still from all those women, bright with need?

4) Three Brothers

My father's brothers stand across the road,
behind them is the pub, they call to him:
'Time for a quick one, come on Les, just one,'
and as they speak he's with them in the dim
cool of the bar-room. It's as if grief's load
had quickly and unexpectedly gone,

while snug between the hunting pictures and
the cigarette machine each holds his drink,
teasing their brother, coughing, laughing hard.
'It's time you left, boy.' But my dad can't think
why Uncle Jack says that or shakes his hand
until he stops, outside the pub's facade.

5) Mother Kindness

Mother kindness, rough red hands,
a house as dizzy as a cold,
your mole dark rooms and snuffling humour,
your creaking swing where I lost my hold.

I stalked my cousin through the grass
and in a green and clumsy bed

travelled the brightness of her legs
while treetops hissed above my head.

Mother kindness, rough red hands,
you shouted down your cats and birds
and scrubbed my face with mother-spit,
I gagged and laughed and screamed for words.

WELL SPOKEN

Her husband's books, still shelved in every room,
remained as ghosts from his profession:
speech therapist, a trainer of nerve-ridden clergy
made fit for Sunday service by declaiming
the balanced rhymes of noble Georgian poets.

'Breakfast is prompt at eight' and for a term
we shared her over-spacious table, trying
to like each other. 'Can my girlfriend visit?'
I asked off-hand, expecting her consent.
'Oh no, that wouldn't do,' she murmured quickly.

Later that week I stammered out my notice.
'You signed a contract.' While she stood, so frail
and in the right I couldn't find an answer,
well-spoken spirits from those books reproached me,
their drained and decent faces tense with sorrow.

LONDON POEMS

1) New Cross

Inconsequential as the pub we sat in,
our happiness adrift on beer and jokes,
we heard the rasp of rush-hour traffic scraping
the sunstruck street while, ardent through the smoke

of cigarettes you've really given up,
your hands recount a girlhood of divisions:
your family half here, half in the States,
yourself half-Jewish, snared between vocations:

a dissertation on *The Waste Land*, journals
and poetry too personal to publish ...
Washing my hands I catch my sodden face
blurring to middle age in the mirror's tarnish

and know your marine eyes, your recklessness
and repetitions hold no hope of harbour.
You kiss my cheek and take a cab. In sunlight
too strong and oversweet to bear, a liqueur

burning my lungs and softening my mind,
I skirt the fuming cars and turning face
the overblown Victorian hall behind;
above the portal where two Tritons coil

the sun enflames the golden weathervane
crowned by a Jason's ship too long at sea,

its crew of antique heroes barely sane,
drunk on the promise of an Empire's spoil.

2) Otherwise

You shaved your head and tried to put on weight
because the men who touched your body were
contemptible, a stale, intrusive blur.
But still your cultured voice would captivate

new friends until you'd hear yourself express
your repetitious rage in one stark speech:
rapid, unstoppable and searing each
numb word with such unguessable distress.

Today I saw you handing leaflets out,
disowned by everyone your voice still rang
down Regent Street, unsullied by self-doubt:

in crimson silks, triumphant and absurd,
you danced from soul to dazzled soul and sang
but to a tune no sane man ever heard.

3) Cloakroom Attendant

The sadness of big buildings brews in me,
I am divorced by space and yet attendant on
the murmur of the rich. My shift half done
I face these hours with a trained passivity.

The subdued light reflects against the glass
and past the potted ferns I see the white
glimmer of laughing guests; perhaps I'll write
a letter home or watch the waiters pass

or sit and read, five floors above the Thames,
nerveless and patient as a block of wood
(and why should I complain, the tips are good).
So many subjects here, potential themes:

the guard with thinning hair who treads his round
his walkie-talkie crackling in his grip,
the over-skinny girl who stops to slip
a compact from her purse without a sound,

intent upon a face she must restore,
before she joins her crowd. I slowly sift
the details out: the lovers by the lift
flirt while they wait, about to try some more

secluded bars. And here I spend my days.
Two couples bring their tags and leaving drop
a trail of coins across the countertop.
I nod in thanks and briefly meet their gaze.

4) From the Chapel

Almost eleven and the station fills
with couples staring down the lines of track,
a soldier strokes his girlfriend's back,
waiting in frost to hear the whining wheels,

a drunk is swearing with deliberate care
and from the chapel, bright, large-hatted, black,
three women dizzy on a gust of prayer
sing Jesus, Jesus on the brittle air.

A small man reads the news and mouths each word,
his lips consume a famine and a war
and still the women sing, each nodding head

dazed with a vision of that joy deferred
beyond the graves of their impoverished dead
while we, the other travellers, numbly stare.

5) Theatre Usher

While Hamlet swears that readiness is all,
sneaking towards the fire escape I blink
against the sudden light and reach the small
balcony, looking out across the black

and trembling surface of the Thames. I hear
the numb, unending surge of shining cars
across the bridge. About a distant pier
a thread of lights promotes a choice of bars

aboard a ship that never leaves its place.
I let the sudden coolness clear my mind,
my hands tight on the rail, the curbless space
a soothing respite from the hot, confined

and breathing darkness where the silent rows,
intent on one man's sorrow on a stage,
dip to the light and smile, while others doze,
conquered by boredom, heavy meals or age

until they jolt up, frightened by applause.
(I'll give myself five minutes then go back.)
Tracing above the moulting sycamores
the pinched Germanic spires of Temple, black

even against the night, and Charing Cross,
a space-age fortress lit in white and green,
I nurse my patience, curb a sense of loss
that comes more often now, and stand unseen

but happy on that damp concrete until
I take my seat before the curtain call:
watching the courtiers circle for the kill
while Hamlet swears that readiness is all.

6) More Soldiers

The Thames still weaves its silver threads
beneath the throbbing helicopters;
they want more soldiers and the daughters
of Sunday idlers skip, it needs

a steady beat to dodge the rope,
it needs a steady heart to watch
the double-blades returning catch
the Greenwich sun. My horoscope

predicts an easy week. I fold
the paper over and so meet
our leader's endless gaze. It's sweet

to watch the tour boats pass, to dip
among used books. I am too old
to nurse this rage. The children skip.

7) Home Through Camden

The drunks and beggars shout each other down,
a lash of light, the kebab stalls, the smart
and shaven bouncers by their doors, and drawn
to certain clubs, the girls who make crowds part,

unworldly seers with a far-off stare,
the Goths and pseudo-vampires gliding past,
defiant, for a time, at Time, aware
that immortality will never last.

I dip beyond them all, past patient queues
and men that stagger on their girlfriends' arms,
the screams of lovers and of car alarms

towards the black canals and formal Mews,
then to the silence of our planned estate,
my concrete stillness where your letters wait.

NIGHT SONGS

1) Making Sense

A man is looking at nine photos dealt
like cards across a cafe table: six
are simply seascapes with a mound
of grass as foreground, nothing else
but clouds above the washed-out tide,
a girl is in the other three.
It's getting late, two waiters stare,
he moves the photos patiently
as if there were a pattern here
logic alone could never state:
the girl, the sea, the frowning waiters;
he tries again, it's getting late.

2) Pat

A smear of blood across the stairway wall,
the keys still in the lock, that holy smile
of unconcern, the skinny body small
and getting smaller: 'Give me just a while … '

No telltale reek, the vodka odourless,
replacing food, the dropless bottle thrown
at a reproachful fox, a helplessness
subsumed in humour and a maudlin groan

before he struck the sofa. His reward
for quitting work: two weeks of drink to show
he didn't care. One midnight hour, I heard

his tales: a marriage out of pregnancy,
long, loveless ... how his sister met a slow
death on the street ... he sipped on endlessly.

3) Background Radio

Ten years of sorrow, not conspicuous,
he worked, met girls, but then it seemed someone
had left a radio forever on
across the street, not noticed in the press
of talk or newfound love but always there.
At last the only thing he heard: a drone
that took his days, then her, then every prayer.

4) His Swans

'Each year the swans stop there to nest, each year
the bastards smash the eggs.' You tap your beer
and point across the canal's moss-green stretch
to where two silent yellow diggers perch
like storks on what was once a block of flats.
'Now everyone has gone; I'm hoping that's
good for the birds.' You smile your charming smile
(the diggers growl again) and shift a pile
of manuscripts, unread and waiting for
your swift unerring touch – as firm and sure

as that constraint which makes you live alone.
(No lover lasts, in comic monotone
you list their flaws but keep your hopes alive.)
Now with the dusk the stupid swans arrive.

5) Night Stroll

A drunk is shrugging, full
of comic disbelief
at his condition and
the market men have packed
their stalls up for the night.

More rain, the lurch and fall
of one unlikely leaf,
a beggar's outstretched hand,
denials and the stacked
boxes in the amber light.

A long walk back through this,
lost to intelligence,
by sleeping bags beside
the yawning shops, cars pass
in hushed serenity.

Two huddled figures kiss
with hungry negligence;
I do not break my stride
but wonder what it is
that has its tooth in me.

THE WOODS

A whirl of trees, the urgent second goes,
a crack of branches in the cool half-dark,
remote the dazzle of the sun on bark,
      nutshells and mud on loosened clothes.

I pull the nettles from our makeshift track,
we reach the fields and stumble into air
swayed by the afterbeat of what we were,
      the beech trees stirring at our back.

BAD SCRIPT, GOOD FILM

Which Hammer Horror was it, where we saw
Christopher Lee despairing at the script
and visibly embarrassed by his lines,
explaining when the evil wizard died
and when the heroine leapt back to life:
'The spell of death rebounded on its maker
and everything that happened ... didn't happen'?

We were aficionados of the bad
and rolled about the sofa, cackling at
this Very Special Gem, before we found
new reasons for our laughter and our rolling.
The evil wizard died. We clung to irony
and knew that bad was good, much like our kisses,
then everything that happened ... didn't happen.

CHILD MINDING

Her daughters in their sickness loll
across the sofa, careless of their tall
and awkward minder, here because
their parents found nobody else
with time to spare. I clear up spilt
juice and then rearrange a quilt
that scarcely needs it. Once I loved
their mother; bored at school we proved
our depth by writing anguished letters
then moved on. Now the sunlight falters
across her living room, I gaze
at photos snapped on holidays:
a smiling couple on the snow,
a dodgem ride, the girls I know
as frowning babies dressed in white.
Heading towards a frosty night
I wait for her return and keep
my counsel while her daughters sleep.

INDIRA'S LAUNDRY

You cry because the clothes you washed are flecked
with shredded tissue, spilt from a nightgown's pocket,
because you were so tired you didn't check

and more you cry from shame, perturbed that such
a trivial slip can flood you with such anger:
who else has fought so hard against bad luck?

You draft your epic lists designed to block
the wasted hour, the ludicrous mistake,
and still you lose your keys. Your bric-a-brac

collects about your shelves: a plastic dragon
picked up on some forgotten childhood jaunt,
a dancing god, a light-bulb and a shell;

each week a new addition witnesses
your sorrows snapping like a family,
protesting that their fury springs from love.

Each night your parents phone to check you're safe,
exiled from Bangladesh, their home burned down,
their voices waver with a fear of rape;

your ruined country and your ruined laundry
forever share the same sardonic world,
you write to me of both. I walk the beach,

uncertain whether I've deserted you,
the sea subdued, the moonlight's flecks of tissue
stinging my eyes, and wonder how to answer.

IN THE CAFE

Two years of age and fascinated by
a shaken set of keys; he wants to catch
the twisting flicker of the offered metal,
while shoppers stop their chat and watch him try
to reach beyond his mother's hand or match
her laughing will with his. Should I forget all

weighty interpretations? Keys are keys
and nothing else. The coffee drinkers care
because the boy is happy in his quest
and needs no other motive, only these
few minutes of desire. The mother's stare
swerves to her watch, they go and leave the rest

of us to take a sip or start our talk again.
Somewhere she puts him in the car and turns
one of her keys. That world of happiness
begins to drive away. A gentle rain
filters the sunlight and the coffee burns
my tongue. Somewhere two lovers will undress.

OUTCLASSED

Pursued by you and caught, I wait each night
in cafes, bars, once by the *Cutty Sark*:
its figurehead that witch, her skin fish-white,
still reaching for her drunkard in the dark.

Late, out of breath, pretending that you ran,
you press against me, tugging at my coat
to make me dip my head. Each night what can
I do but touch your lips or stroke your throat

and huddle to your warmth? Untidy by
your elegant and well-dressed side, your hand
(each nail immaculate) in mine, I try
despite my fuddled mind to understand

why you, twelve years my junior and more
assured than I shall ever be, arrange
these meetings. 'Tell me what you did before
you met me.' Happy in your bed I range

across my memories, my mind still full
of your wild tales. I dodge your begging looks;
your travels and your lovers making dull
my stock reply 'I read a lot of books.'

No doubt you'll leave, because I sometimes fail
in bed, because I can't afford to buy
a single suit you wear. No doubt you'll sail
beyond my reach; I kiss your perfect thigh.

FIRST DAYS

No water pressure and the tub half full,
the shower useless while I shambled from
kitchen to bathroom with a saucepan of

warm water in each hand. You crouched, head bowed,
your long hair smeared with suds, directing me.
I christened you with slow, repeated

downpours. That was our first fortnight in our first
apartment; while the steam obscured the mirror,
your costly tubes of cream, the Mucha print

our predecessor left, you kneaded out
your hair in coils before you left for work.
I wondered what to do next, stopping by

the bedroom door, unsteady in the sunlight,
knowing that something new had started now.
I heard the music of our neighbours and

the shouts of children like the sound of water.

SOCIAL NOTES

1) Fidelity

'Your diligent persistence merits praise
but not from me, when was it mine to give?
You stayed because you had your principles
and swore your covert oath: some day you'd *live*.
Now like a clerk you count the passing days
while TV laughter echoes off the walls;
in bed you kiss, click off the light and turn.
Saint Paul remarked we marry or we burn,
the good man got it wrong – go home and burn.'

2) Advancement

My wife dislikes this and she may be right,
this middle-aged advancement down my back
defying tweezers and each fresh attack
of suds and razor. Weekly now, those tight
black curls traverse my shoulders and my cells
rewrite themselves: 'My love, you're getting old.'
Creased face, white hairs and gradually I've told
myself the metaphors of age: here dwells
my bullish pride, my wolfish disposition,
drool-jawed and snarling at the loss of youth –
crude overstatements surely, not the truth,
not all of it? I meet this beast's attrition
in locked bathrooms, until the mirrors melt
my snow-flecked muzzle and my glossy pelt.

3) This Actor's Laughter

This actor's laughter is a conscious choice,
the head thrown back, the lips retreat and fire
short bursts, each triggered by the same desire
to please directors, agents, those whose voice

is heard in casting circles. Table slaps
are also used, though sparingly because
excess does not persuade. The slightest pause
of hesitation, then that loud collapse

in mirth denotes more wisdom and more taste.
When done, his head remains a turret where
tired troops await the next attack, his stare,

a marksman's, scans the dinner's sodden waste
until his laughter cannonades once more;
avoid that sound, his victims know its roar.

4) Threesome

Two men, one woman and a plot
as basic as their acting skills;
the grappling combinations knot
body to body without rest
and promise non-stop, adult thrills
as each man cups a generous breast.

They struggle in a close-up, each
demanding more while she receives

them with some tenderness, hands reach
for buttocks or to guide a man
to what he faithfully believes
he wants. They end as they began,

separate and looking at each other,
spent and a little puzzled in
a furnished room. Why all this bother,
the hand-held cameras and the need
to mount and then re-mount? They grin
and singly go, as was agreed.

5) Reassuring News

It is well known that women never feel
sexual desire for persons other than
their spouses; virtue and an iron will
make them less fallible than any man.

No woman ever thought *there is no joy*
in marriage or why not seduce a stranger;
or else *I'll give his first time to some boy...*
relax faint-hearted men, there is no danger.

Do not examine bills or buy a gun
or search their nightstands, o you unsure men,
or seek discarded letters just for fun:

I burn for you, my husband is a bore...
You know you're never tedious, so then
return to bed, my tired love, and snore.

6) Examinations

A sharp, suspicious woman's voice
first aimed at me and afterwards
shouting perhaps up darkened stairs,
although I phoned towards midday:
'Thomas,' and with impatience, 'Thomas!'
and next his wispy voice: 'Ah, yes ... '

We marked the English papers quickly
coming to swift agreements, chuckling
at errors, he seemed urbane, informed.
Ending our task, I thought we'd chat,
reflect on teaching, briefly be
something like friends; he cut me short:

'I shouldn't use the phone for long.'
Did 'shouldn't' sound like 'not allowed'?
I wondered if he sat alone
or if the woman stayed beside him,
counting his words like injuries
until she sent him back upstairs.

7) On Running Out of Money

It's strange how quickly
the old solutions
present themselves:
packed lunches in parks,
and free museums
in times of heavy rain

but best to avoid
the bright libraries
where slumped long-timers
will recognise
a growing kinship
you do not want to claim.

8) Staying True

Their married life became a feud,
a summing-up of grievances
that span from vaguest nuances
to outright curses, not just crude
but unforgivable. He must drink
each night, she joined societies –
avoidance of hostilities
seemed a solution; but one blink
will end a life and he went first
(as by statistics men will do).
She chose no other, staying true
to one insensible and cursed.
Such posthumous fidelity
was proved by photos of the pair
smiling on beaches: she still fair
and he incapable of treachery.

SEVEN LOVE POEMS

1) Double Act

Only the phone cord tethered me,
I joked, and stopped me floating off,
airborne with simple happiness;

because the world was serious enough
our love became a levity,
a double act called More and Less.

Ironic that our rapid patter
becomes more weighty and more true
than vows I've sworn in some distress.

One time I trod the air with you
and improvised our subject matter;
wasn't there laughter? More and less.

2) Haytor

The August sunlight baked the tar,
only the shadows kept their cool,
I scampered on from stone to stone

beyond my parents and their car,
more than content to play the fool;
we found our height and there, alone,

I asked if I might marry you.
For you I was a summer fling,
a frolic with a younger man,

an almost boy of twenty-two.
(Somewhere I heard a lapwing sing,
dazed by my words, I had no plan.)

You were so kind, so scrupulous,
refused without rejection's sting
but rather ended with a kiss;

relieved, I felt the summer bless
my lips (no need to buy that ring).
Two decades on, I wish you had said yes.

3) The Airport

After you left I strolled around
and bought a book I've never read;
sometime I knew I'd have to head
back home, no hurry. Having found
the toilets (polished, steel-framed jobs),
I locked the door, put down my book,
recalling your last, smiling look
before I sobbed my first loud sobs,
fiercer by far than your first kiss.
'This must be grief,' I thought, 'just this
stupidity, so dumbly true.'
Another thing I'd learnt from you.

4) Again

Too green, too dense, the summer hours of rain,
while in this torpid park, I stop to find
some private joke of ours possess my mind
I hadn't thought of these ten years. Again

I hear your terrors: you are unloveable
or talentless or have no will to act
or tire your friends. Again I lack the tact
to coax you round. I watch the hard rain fall:

white tulips bend in decimated rows
as on an empty green, unhurried crows
saunter for scraps and through the swollen dark

two mothers with their covered prams appear
laughing and drenched. Again I want you here
and one police car dawdles round the park.

5) Face

She said Don't touch your face.
For twenty years I kept
my sneaking hands away,

swayed by her advice
long after we had swept
our lifelong plans away.

Why is it now I find
these same hands clawing back,
why don't they keep away?

Chin, nose and lips: my mind
plays out its list: a track
of creasing skin, a way

across the territory:
eye sockets, forehead, hair.
Start, middle, end, a way

to plot a tricky story;
I stalk my face through air
before it gets away.

6) Good Advice

1
They said I should work with my hands:
I cleared the back yard, combed the cats for fleas
and fixed the toilet cistern.

The sense of achievement
was underwhelming.

2
They said I should write about you:
I wrote a story full of wit and pathos,
which I consider highly publishable.

I must however add
that literature is no substitute for life.

3
They said I should take long, brisk walks
and get that country air into my lungs.
Whatever you do, do not try this:

I ended up miles from anywhere
with my head full of you.

7) Invocation

I sleepwalk without you,
each day becomes a month,
the months are turned to years;
I sleepwalk without you,
two hours with you are worth
weeks of convulsive tears.

I sleepwalk without you
(two wives, one special friend,
three jobs and several lies);
I sleepwalk without you
and will do to the end,
no need to close my eyes.

I sleepwalk without you
and never quite learned how
to wake unless you're near;
I sleepwalk without you,

I've slept through decades now
and still you are not here.

I sleepwalk without you.

CATS

1) Edgar and Sam

Sam was a starving kitten, nothing more,
beneath a hedge beside a busy road,
with eyes still closed; I nudged an outstretched paw
then scooped him up, a black uncertain load.
Over the months I watched that inkblot grow,
become a snarling scourge of mice, who tore
curtains to rags but held one soul in awe:
a cat who worshipped Edgar Allan Poe.

Milton and Wordsworth, Tennyson and Blake
could not dispel his orphaned savagery,
he terrorised our lane without a break
until I read him 'Annabel Lee';
why did he hesitate, begin a slow
sway as his eyes dilated, half-awake,
how much weird beauty could one feline take,
this cat who worshipped Edgar Allan Poe?

From then our nights were crammed with crime and fear:
a tell-tale heart, malignant dwarves, a tomb
where none would rest; I am prepared to swear
Sam purred with pleasure in the gathering gloom,
a mass of black, his gold-flecked eyes aglow,
his claws unsheathed against my ruined chair,
his whiskers almost brushing my left ear,
that cat who worshipped Edgar Allan Poe.

At last I dreamt that Poe had left the dead
to meet his greatest and least human fan,
he signed the cat's flea collar and read
his most disturbing tales with great élan
and all the time the cat swayed to and fro
while worms and grave mould fell from Edgar's head;
at dawn he crumbled and Sam curled on our bed,
my cat who worshipped Edgar Allan Poe.

2) The Status of the Cat

Schrödinger's mouse is nervous: having heard
the cat is neither dead nor quite alive
but indeterminate – that fearful word
is worse than life or death; one cannot thrive
on doubtfulness. The mouse is free or caught
between those playful claws, depending on
the status of the cat. Now, chilled by thought,
he crouches paralysed, a tiny stone
dropped in an endless sea. Say what you please:
he starves beyond the help of any cheese.

3) Domestic Behaviour

Apparently cats may share
two owners unaware
that both are feeding one
domestic animal;
it's comforting to learn

that cats, like us, are far
from scrupulous and turn
for lovers anywhere.

FOUR PLAYS

1) Reading *King Lear*

Watched by the dragonflies,
the King is sobbing and
he should have thought much more
on this, he should have thought;
the spider's gentleness
can make a hedgerow home.

Under the Kentish skies
the small deer graze the land;
the King's a fool, he swore
against the female naught
and conjured barrenness
into a daughter's womb.

Now where the French fleet lies
the crows disturb the strand
but who defends the poor?
This kingdom's dearly bought,
we hear the calf's distress,
the King will die quite soon.

2) Cassandra

My eyes are not my own,
cursed by an angry lover
they saw the slaughter done,

a city overthrown;
I could not run for cover.

Now past his wife I glide
(no shelter from her hate)
and still I cannot hide
but joyful as a bride
approach the narrow gate.

3) Wedding Day

On my brother's wedding day
as I lectured on Shakespeare
and the playing field succumbed
to its muddy emptiness,
marriage thoughts still made their way
past the nodding students, numbed
by the heater's burning paint
or November's dreariness;
while my brother's vows rise, clear
of the years of lone constraint.

Half the globe away, in silk
smiles his bride, a Buddhist priest
eating rice to bless them both,
each king lies to gain his ends ...
in a temple white as milk.
Afterwards the fish and broth
with my parents tense, lost to wonder,
they have servants but no friends ...
promise of a first child feast
gratitude gives way to plunder ...

Falstaff dies as England dies ...
Sleepless night, the willow sighs
buffeted, the level roof
shivers in the downpour, I
watch through glass the twisted skies,
ask what vow or tendered proof
of my love could mend our break.
May you keep your joy, I spy
your new bride, known through your eyes,
leaving her home for your sole sake.

4) Ajax to Odysseus

Spilt oxen blood can not appease my spirit:
you glitter in my armour like a god,
I walk the riverbank and find it odd
how smooth talk steals the prize from silent merit.

Each night the trucks deliver barrelled oil
less slick than you; my madness gone, I hear
the rigging shudder and the cranes change gear
as other wars bring in a different spoil.

No doubt the generals keep some men like you
for Expediters, nimble-tongued and bright
enough to sidestep trouble. Let your bread

be thrown to other ghosts and may you rue
your plausibility. It is not right
to harm a noble man, alive or dead.

GERMANY

1) The Escape

The windows face a rundown central square:
squat snow-clouds and the bookshops. Hours alone,
his body slants across a littered stair:
'I'm looking for a children's book, unknown

to bibliophiles.' He scowls half childish now,
dining on cheese and grapes, a cheap red wine
to keep the winter off. He does not know
the tanks are near, ignores the grand design

changing the colours on an out-sized map.
An epigram defeats his enemies,
rehearsed but fresh, the perfect verbal slap
across time's face. The dust still makes him sneeze.

He has an article to finish, sure
to put an academic in his place,
exposing foggy thinking with the pure
light of a clear style. Suddenly all space

turns snarling on its tail. A gentleman
is calling and his eyes hide other eyes:
'Who are you sir to make me drop my pen?'
'The soldiers are so close, I have my spies,

you are not safe.' That steady smile, a mite
apologetic, the buzz of flies, reveal

a calmness close to absence. So, in spite:
'I need no help.' 'Let me explain the deal…'

Early next morning comes the doorframe's crash,
the notes are checked, a shrug, a backward look.
Two crows fly past a chimney belching ash,
the snow hills open like a children's book.

2) The Golem

Dark streets, sleepwalker step, a doughy face,
the Rabbi's clay man with the single word,
Emeth for truth scratched on his brow, absurd
and mute with little memory; erase

one letter and he halts, becoming death:
a motionless grotesque, each block-like hand
clenched as with grief. He will not understand
complex commands, they are a waste of breath,

but ambles on indifferent to the order:
bring gold, save us from soldiers, burn and ravage
this evil land. All's one to him. Let mad

men rage or sane men cry, he will not falter
while we, alas, are like a magpie's plumage,
neither entirely good or wholly bad.

3) Kinder

Knowing you will not know: the children play
all morning with a ball and others watch
silent beyond a tricky game of catch;
those villages were emptied in a day.

Wide rivers where a single boatman sings
and only willows rise above the marsh,
stirring like gratitude. Somewhere a harsh
siren begins. Should we forget these things?

Recall instead the ancient festivals,
the hopeful girls in white, the crude red wine,
the drunken card-games where the gentry lose

and do not mind. The talking animals
saw soldiers laughing on the borderline;
sometimes the dead would mend their children's shoes.

4) Her Grandparents

That night they found another thirteen fleas
between their blankets, while his countrymen
prowled through the woods for collaborators
(they had his name) and hers had just begun
to be de-Nazified. She piled their plates
and shivered at his side in loyal silence
among the corpses of those thirteen fleas.

5) Grossmütter

You waved the Kaiser past;
three years old, deafened by
the beefy, cheering crowd,

perhaps that was your last
hour of security
although you were too proud

to mutter, bore the yoke
of jealous father and
of faithless husband, spared

nothing. One tongue, one folk
but who would understand
those wrongs you left unshared:

your grown son's mental age
a child's, your artist's skill
withered? You coaxed a slow

expenditure of rage
through ninety years and still
you watch the final Kaiser go.

6) Local Wines

These are the cautious days, the Thames itself
is vexed, suspicious, locked in its own path

beneath our commerce and our schemes for wealth,
I write despite myself then laugh:

'This plenitude of words will win me nothing,
better the silence of a crafty man,
better the daily test of watching, noting,
the stealthy nursing of a long held plan.'

But wasn't there another time when I
first climbed those unsafe steps above the pines
with Germany and France all promised past

that shattered castle and the August sky,
back when I thought that joy would surely last,
sharper and stronger than the local wines?

EAST COAST

1) Kent

County of tired commuters curbed by frost,
of dawn-light golfers and of camping parks,
of ancient boundaries and stale bunkers lost
to brambles where the exclamation marks

of children stutter through a soldier's game;
your histories are written in the eyes
of loud, mascaraed girls – there, tales of shame
and dead adulterers stir no surprise

to stall the traffic of our fished-out seas.
Beneath cathedrals, tiny pubs disgorge
football fans, lovers and flushed pensioners

(sparks flicker still about a rusted forge);
while something perilous, an old disease
still grips your fighters and your mariners.

2) Margate

Old world, perhaps: white houses by the sea,
the shops which may reopen in the spring,
even the clubs embrace stability:
the smoking boys, the laughing girls who sing
the latest hits against the winter gale,
an interlude of joy then home to tea.
 Their young replace them without fail.

Enduring and endurable the town
protects its saucy mothers and the mild
drunks by the bandstand; we cannot disown
the needle in the street or frightened child.
Our strength is our survival; we watch the ships,
heavy with cargo, pass, enjoy the wild
　　　world circling and our own eclipse.

Old women talk of when a summer's crowd
would clog the coast, some comic's punning speech
bewitched the closed theatres; we were proud.
Defeat like perfume soughs across the beach,
the wind performs a Pierrot's drab routine;
lovers no longer pay to laugh aloud.
　　　I cross my town's historic green.

3) Our Ghosts

Nothing to fear: no spooks on stairs
or messages in mirror glass,
no sudden shrieks or gothic gloom,

only the poise of empty chairs
or someone near, about to pass
in hallways or a silent room

and not just one: a couple or
a family, not hostile, tired
even bewildered, kept too late

and looking for the proper door
to slip away; the wife required
to bear with grace this puzzling fate,

soothes her scared husband while they wait.

4) Commuting on Christmas Eve

Keeping my counsel in the Christmas dark,
I take the city train, the unlit fields
peel back to farms and villages, the folds
of riverbanks by factories, I drink
silence and coffee while the carriage fills.

Distrusting all the rhetoric of faith,
my cards unwritten and my book unread,
I nurse my idleness until some fault
of rail or plan suspends us on our road
with nothing out there for the eye to find.

Now with the engine stopped, the lighting dimmed,
I hear the song: a blackbird's stubborn call
dispelling stillness, making its demand
of guessed-at valleys, networks in the chill
of nowhere; then we stir, the day's cold dream

drags us from vacancy, I think again
of Midnight Mass this evening and the church
I link with school, something I thought outgrown
with cardboard crowns and other props I clutched
while marching blindly in a home-made gown.

5) Dead Crabs

The winter cold had killed
the crabs and dragged them back,
their plates and claws no shield
against that slow attack;
what numbness had they let
invade them stealthily,
what cause here for regret –
why waste my sympathy?
Seagulls surveyed that wealth:
hinged shells and emptied eyes
and I, despite myself,
wished death were otherwise.

6) Omens

Again I think of omens such as crows,
God's writing on the sky; did Plato claim
such birds had guts so we might read the future –

a hidden code? Unlikely, I suppose
although today I'd cling without much shame
to any theory out of man or nature

to bring you back unharmed. I scour the trees
for magpies, try to spot my 'joyful' two,
the hospital behind me now. I'll get the call

this afternoon but still, search how I please,
God's hand eludes me. Just the usual view:
a corner shop and kids approaching school.

OTHER TRAVELS

1) The Waiting Room

The women smoking and their shopping bags
around their feet; a bright fruit machine spells
its patterns out in light and on the walls
a map, hygiene certificates, two flags,

a sun-spent picture called 'The Peaceful Lake':
all bric-a-brac that found no other home
except a railway tea-room. Far from harm
the children pester mothers for some cake

and I am near to tears. November light
wavers against the far wall while I drink
my viscous coffee, shaping rhymes to link
this pattern into words. I hear the lilt

of Welsh on English in this border town;
one young girl slams carnations on the tables,
one to a jar, some white, some red, each trembles
on impact while I write the details down

because this cannot last. A crowd begins
to gather, others leave. I check my watch
and push around the ashtray one charred match
while at the fruit machine a thin man wins.

2) Winter Tourists

I grin beside the gates to Rydal Mount
(closed for the winter) waiting for the flash
and driving off we heard the body count
was rising hourly from the German crash:

three Britons dead among a random crowd
from different nations on a single train.
The heartless silver of the lake still prowled
beside our dawdling car; we stopped again

to take the ferry over Ullswater.
Free from the news, beyond our radio,
we hugged, not from romance but from the cold,

the mountains folding round us and the air
charged with the promise of an early snow;
we held each other tight and kept our hold.

3) The Octopus

Clop, clop, clop and we wake to watch
a fisherman beside a rock
smashing an octopus, his catch
and livelihood. The aftershock

pursues as round the disused fort
the Turks once won from Venice, now
weeds, cats and lizards own the court
and burn beneath the grinding blow

of morning sunlight. Over gift
shops and the early season stir
of torpid restaurants, we lift
our gaze beyond the mosque to where,

a map of snow, the mountain range
floats like some folk-tale sorceress
or like a fortune-teller, strange,
absurd, foretelling happiness.

ART LESSONS

1) Waterhouse and the Tempest

One of his last depicts her on a coast
of shattered stone. She grips her damp red hair
with one smudged hand. No palms or glowing dunes
but Cornish granite traps the cobalt air,

the sea an oily swell, a fractured mast
stirs doglike at her feet. Her durable
blue dress, red-cuffed, resists this British gale.
Drenched in an upper corner of his work

a model ship is coaxed towards the rocks.
In childish print another corner offers
his name and year of painting: nineteen-sixteen.
Whiter than fresh drawn sap she stares and suffers

with those that she saw suffer: sailors lost
and drowned, almost, before her father's word
subdues the storm and lulls them gently home.
The artist, sixty-seven and one year

from death by cancer, holds no magic wand
to quell the thunder. He reads this morning's list
of casualties and mouths each fading name,
his aching bulk sunk in a garden chair,

his style of art unfashionable, threadbare
and even maudlin; while that girl, the same

in all his pictures, treads towards the tide
and hears no music on the tainted air.

2) In Defence of Realism

Fidelity is virtuous perhaps,
each leaf is numbered and each feather blessed
while through a sheep's ear the sunlight strays;
such work is visible, it shows no lapse
in hurried corners, all this world addressed
with equal love. There's something here to praise.

Let's take the people in that stringent field:
we know their earnings and their social class
in seconds and a single look betrays
a silent jealousy. The bluff, unskilled
lover talks on and beauty smiles. All will pass
before the harvesting of autumn days.

Easy to deride such a scrupulous
approach as unimaginative, drained
of deeper meaning, as another craze
for literalness but any lover knows
this joy in such particulars. It rained,
the picnic party left, their promise stays.

3) Ingmar Bergman

The doomed musician plays his final song,
upstairs the children suffer and tell tales,

a toy theatre chronicles what's wrong,
outside the nursery a marriage fails.

Worn down by art and cunning, by small crimes,
women fall mute beside the level shore
and ageing men recall their braver times:
black horses in white foam and nothing more.

It should be easy, like a summer fling,
hopping between the islands, bellies full
of sex and stolen food; why should we face

the journey back, the lawyers and the sting
of loss? Not easy, irresponsible.
One woman sobs. Whose is the next embrace?

IN MEMORY OF PETER LEVI

'You want to be a poet?' and the grin,
'Good man!' The champagne brandished with a toast,
three hours of drinking while you bellowed praise
(as if possessed by some berserker's ghost)

of Shakespeare, Pasternak and obscene puns
found on the walls of Spanish lavatories:
'Such poetry!' A crazed bank manager,
deskbound but drunk on vast analogies;

you stopped and peered towards the fresh-washed green
of Oxford fields: 'I've got a class to teach ... '
Tweed-clad, bull-backed, thin-legged you reared
        and charged
while I, unsteady, near deprived of speech,

I knew myself a poet in that hour,
your alcohol still crooning in my blood.
On later days you read my teenage verse,
dismissing dull lines with the words 'dead wood'.

Today I gathered up your final letters
where, always kind, you wrote while you were cast
adrift by blindness ('just like Milton'); dying
you wondered if your poetry would last.

No need to wonder now. I mouth your words,
their tense, laconic strength untouched by doubt,
as certain as the small and swift woodpecker,
this dazzling chilly morning, drumming out

its message on our dry and rotten branches;
as if it too had heard and understood
your gruff, unerring voice, your ceaseless message:
'Remove dead wood, always remove dead wood.'

DEAD STOCK

The books that haven't sold a copy in
one year become dead stock; we pry them out,
the shelves must work, these texts achieve a bin

or distant warehouse (something said about
'tax purposes'). We ease them from our lists,
just rarely stopping with a flare of doubt

beside a pile of Irish dramatists
or some biography that tells you how
an East End life was lived 'with joy, with fists,

with heart'. Perhaps we'll keep a few, we know
we shouldn't but a flicker of affection
towards an author's photograph will slow

us for a moment. Hope invites reflection:
those eyes are desperate for enduring fame
or if not that at least due recognition.

We read the back: a blurb from some big name,
a stately font, a novel's silly plot
or some philosopher's almighty claim

to mend the world with thought. We briskly jot
a number down, return to our last spot
and sift the nameless from the soon forgot.

UNCOLLECTED POEMS & LAST POEMS

BANGLADESH 1977

That winter famine was the worst in years,
an orphanage of shrunken babies, live
enough to watch a land remote from tears:
'Give food to those who cry, they might survive,

the silent ones already know they are dead.'
Dumbstruck by all that would not happen for them
each mute child turned his small and worried head,
no one to nurture, coddle, or adore them.

Do small children die small deaths? I do not know.
Smallest of babies, half your proper size, the
dwindling ward re-echoed to your cries.

You won the food the others were denied,
adopted, you outlived them long ago
but still the silent ones press to your side.

* Included in pamphlet *Waterhouse and the Tempest*
but not *The Status of the Cat.*

BEFORE THE INTERVIEW

Watching the sparrows skirmish in the trees
and waiting for another interview –
a change of life? God knows it's overdue.
The academics rage about a pay review:
One must be cynical... A Japanese
garden beyond their gossip greets the breeze.
I hear the sound of water and pretend
I have a perfect mastery of Zen.

Near fifty now and hunting for a post
whose title starts with 'senior', I leave my table;
both publishing and perishing, now lost
somewhere between 'notable' and 'not able',
I catch the flicker of a dragonfly
then find the Gents and knot my bright blue tie.

BIRD SHIT

A gentle tap like fingers
against my turning shoulder –
only the hedge – my shirt
stippled with purple juice:
bird shit? No stink, the sun
bleaching the fields of Kent.

Lying awake this morning
I thought of walking out
on both my house and life;
I'd take a ferry trip
to France, tank up on brandy
and chance the night-bound sea.

Later I put on my
washed shirt and noticed where
the berry juice had left
a trail of greenish spots.
Didn't someone say
that bird shit meant good luck?

BLISS

The monks in Soho
are chanting; one laughs with joy
at a passing car.

I'm unconvinced;
even Buddhists in their bliss
include bad actors.

THE BOAT RIDE

The waves and bathers' shouts became a hush;
I picked through marram grass and yellow wort
by seagull feathers rotting in a bush
to where those cries dispersed. I tried to sort

the details out: smudged primrose on the dunes,
a magpie at the margin of my thought
and weeds that cluttered up a track of stones.
I found the torpid pool where sunlight caught

the flickering progress of a dragonfly
and, stopping, watched awhile. Beyond the call
of herring-gull and tern, I crouched to spy
the slightest movement in that marsh: the small

tremors of water boatmen on the tight
skin of the pond. This was the final place
I always knew I'd reach: no appetite
remaining, nothing but a ledge of space,

my last ambitions gone, my heart stripped bare.
My mind, a boatman on that absolute Now,
sailed out from definition, time and care;
the waves were tame against that cleaving prow.

I was the last colonial and swept
towards the tropics where the sunlight ends,
no cargo slowed me down although I kept
just one regret: no cabin room for friends.

CHILDERMASS ACROSTIC

His name denotes a kind of over-acting.
Even today we 'out-Herod Herod',
Ridicule appeals when watching tyrants
Opining that they know the will of God,
Denouncing 'liberals', strutting their defiance;

Laughter is one response to such bad acting.
It makes us more secure, more comfortable.
Victory seems assured against a fool.
Each day more people, we suspect, are able –
Surely? – to see the madness of his rule.

True, but what if they love such madcap acting?
Our satire stops when children start to die,
Debris and rape are part of his performance
And there are always encores. Watch the sky.
Yes, he always finishes with a dance.

CREAM

The cat that got the cream does not purr,
she is discreet and goes about her business
while others moan around the garden fence.

Theft is the better option: not for her
our 'yours' and 'mine'. She hears a neighbour's voice:
My husband has to work so late, I guess ...

THE FRAGILE DAUGHTERS

I miss the fragile daughters of the rich
with all their part-time jobs and full-time dreams,
training to dance or act, prepared to switch
from course to course while still one vision gleams
beyond negotiations and phone-calls:
'Two hours I fought with Daddy, but he seems
to understand … ' The cheque arrives, the walls
resound with projects for 'a truly new
theatre, radical enough to cause
the damned Establishment to choke, turn blue
and die, it only needs one well-timed blow … '
Months pass, she rents a villa with a view
and nothing's staged. Where do those young girls go?
Some marry, some sell sandwiches or bitch
about Artistic Differences. I know
of one who builds birdhouses, others ditch
us all and disappear, a handful throw
their lives away: 'I scorn a world in which … '
I miss the fragile daughters of the rich.

FROM MY BEDROOM

At 5.30 in the morning
I hear laughter from the doorway
of the casino.

I do not know whether
the laughing is triumphant
or rueful.

Twenty minutes later
all I can hear is the whirr
of the air-conditioning.

GIRAFFE

Standing far from the crowd
as if made twice as strong
by heroic loneliness,
his fragile head so proud
of everything gone wrong.

Without a place to rest
and overqualified,
he wears his helplessness
like medals on his breast
with heart-destroying pride.

Where did he make the first
of many errors, why
wouldn't he see the mess,
the desert years, the thirst,
the wives bent down to cry?

Long legs, high mind and never
much cash, he plagues each friend
for loans until we bless
the spiteful rows that sever
our friendship and the end

we will not have to watch,
far off or far too near,
the night when weariness
will mute him and he'll pass
on stilts and full of fear.

HIJACKING THE POETRY CLASS

I tell my class that poets hold two views:
'Most claim all's for the best and we become
stronger by error but a few refuse
this comfort; being stubborn, or just dumb,

they argue for a primal sin, a choice
we made which closed the gates of paradise,
we'll never hear again the lost one's voice,
our souls forever caged in cells of ice ... '

Some students realise that para-rhymes
no longer form our topic; Grumpy stirs,
the Sweet Girl smiles. I talk and watch the floor,

' ... but is that "never" really true? Sometimes,
the utterly impossible occurs:
that woman waited for / walks through the door.'

JENKINTOWN, PA

A squirrel skittered on the roof,
dislodged the ice in one long sheet
to shatter on the dripping street.
The impact echoed on the rough

stone of the Catholic Church and school,
as, coming from the liquor store,
I felt your town begin to thaw
so unexpectedly that all

the road was wet with mirrored light;
squinting, I foresaw our last break
but reached your parents' home to make
the wedding plans and book our flight.

LONG DISTANCE

I end my shift and catch the night bus, lapse
to blankness while the amber lights play on
the dug-up streets; I watch the lorries turn
for new supplies and taste our near collapse.

No living contact and the silence saps
our resolution; now your parents phone
suggesting you'd go further on your own,
each gentle sentence starting with Perhaps ...

They'll say that you were right to finish this,
congratulate you on the wisest choice
and they'll be wrong. Perhaps no one could miss

my lack of money or my lost career;
you'll find your plenty elsewhere. But my voice
will break your sleep, distant and always near.

THE MAGICIAN'S WIFE

Coins tumbled from her ear,
never such wealth! Then more:
an egg came from a glove,
symbol of hope and fear,
roses appeared before
an ectoplasmic love.

Shared warmth of bodies told him
she'd stay through thick and thin;
she watched the stage clock tick:
no chain could ever hold him,
no prison lock him in,
but marriage did the trick.

While underwater he
smiled in his tank and eased
the handcuffs from his wrist,
determined to be free,
unborn her baby, pleased
by precept, clenched a fist.

Then like any mother
she saw how it was done,
she felt her courage fail:
vanishing loved ones offer
no solace once they've gone
like droplets in a pail
and widowed she'd recall
his greatest trick of all.

MALEDICTION ON CRITICAL THEORY

Tell the academies I will not speak
in service any longer; let those willing
inform the credulous and young, the weak
or hesitant, all life is text and killing
is just a sign, the victims signifiers.
The lecture rooms (where other voices now
recite those sacred names, their cautious vow
designed to stifle chance, the reckless fires
of youth and daring) should be sealed until
all recognise that stones are stones, that water
cleanses or drowns and words excuse no slaughter,
that wounds bleed more than words and surgeons heal.
This world is not inside a scholar's head,
tell the academies their words are dead.

MARGATE IN AUGUST

Past where kestrels hover
over motorways
plays each child and lover
on their holidays;
gone the nights of worry,
flurry of the waves
saves us from the fury
of our waiting graves.

While the tan grows deeper
sleeper and swimmer rest,
best to stay (and cheaper)
with our bodies pressed
close to one another;
other bathers shout
out to kids or mother
or scan the sky with doubt.

Coast of burns and lollies,
follies large and small,
all with breaks and brollies
pitched against a squall —
never lose your kindness,
your blindness to our faults;
ports like this unbind us
from work and school reports.

MEZZO CAMMIN

My middle year if I am Biblical
(but people live much longer now) no grey,
some laughter lines while I recall today
the promise I was meant to have at school;

I don't know when it drifted out of reach,
when I first felt, as year succeeded year,
this slow declension of my hopes. Now here
I've settled, wordless on a winter beach.

'You need to talk to people,' but I hate
to dance attendance on the not-so-great,
better to trek towards a rockbound pool,

this birthday, checking what the tide forgot:
a damaged buoy, a plastic lobster pot
and other spoils I've sought since leaving school.

THE MIGRATION

Two hundred miles she came, so brave and lost,
to save our marriage, hopeless from the first
but still we took the path along the coast;
we found our way across the Warren's spur
and neither of us noticed how the air
was tense with wailing (when did they appear,
those first few birds?), next growing flocks of starlings
all turning and descending, still more starlings,
and suddenly the sky was full of starlings
weighing the scrub trees down, coming south
in tired droves and barely space enough
between the leaves to hold them, every mouth
shrieking to guide the latest comers in,
their every arc in thoughtless unison.
Amazed, she walked away to watch alone
head back, her lips apart and lost for words
(estranged from me by more than simple yards)
her whole attention on those gusts of birds
that dusk as flocks of starlings interwove
preparing, with a nearness much like love,
to leave the worst of winter, not to starve.

MORE STATUES PLEASE

Statues leap up: for animals that fall
in time of war, for artists with cravats,
the Queen unveils a statue to herself;
let there be seating sculptors, filling all
the city parks beneath the circling bats
(there's more than money to a nation's wealth).

Next we must celebrate the heroes gone
because our smiling leader needs a war
to illustrate 'self evident' ideals;
immortalise the hooded young, each done
for theft, now circling a silver car
on mountain bikes, still turning, wheels on wheels.

Far from tower-blocks, each name a town
(Sherborne and Stratford, Arundel or Rye),
some lonely, tearful soldier goes berserk,
possessed by England's glittering renown,
he'll need a statue too, Lest Honour Die:
my countrymen, let's give those sculptors work.

* Included in pamphlet *Waterhouse and the Tempest*
but not *The Status of the Cat.*

MY GERMAN GRANDMOTHER REMEMBERS

'And they were vain and silly girls
blessed with more gallantry than sense,
practising pouts, arranging curls,
they giggled and scaled the farmyard fence.

'blessed with more gallantry than sense,
all three had beaus and loved to flirt,
they giggled and scaled the farmyard fence;
if they took chances, who was hurt?

'All three had beaus and liked to flirt
but what do warplanes know of art,
if they took chances who was hurt?
We piled their bodies in a cart.

'But what do warplanes know of art?
White-faced the farmer saw his girls,
we piled their bodies in a cart
and dragged them past where the river curls.

'White-faced the farmer saw his girls
practising pouts, arranging curls;
we dragged them past where the river curls
but they were vain and silly girls.'

NAPLES

The gods have tumbled
and the trumpet players
have taken the square –
a dispensation
I would gladly vote for.

Across the night
the Bourbons gallop
on stone horses
while the police lounge
in their riot gear.

Street traders ask
if I'd like a rose
for the lovely lady?
No, the lady prefers
limoncello.

Grandiloquent
And graffitied,
despised by tidy
citizens, you live
on your pretensions;

I owe a debt to you
for your lewdness, patience,
and especially for
your trumpet players
wooing us with schmaltz.

NOT TOO BADLY

'You haven't done too badly when you take
account of where you're from,' this with a squeeze
of my held hand. She saunters with the ease
of ballet and good schools. A coffee break

later she's off to shop. I leave my book
to curl in sunlight on the table, watch
the couples pass and try again to catch
the taste of where I'm from: my father's look

behind the butcher's counter, soft, amused,
the gentlest man I know; my mother loud,
using her classroom voice around the place,

recounting sitcom plots like one amazed
at TV's endless wealth and through the crowd
my wife comes back like one possessed with grace.

OLD FOX

Louche grin, saggy belly,
pausing under the street light
and leaving without hurry
when I approach my front door –
what do I owe him?
But still
I end up circling the house,
ham in my half-frozen hand
so I might throw it at him
and watch that slouching silence
step towards me through the snow.

ON THE DEATH OF A COLLEAGUE

On the last day of her life she notices
a yellow ball in a car park.
The jogger on the beach thinks only
of the cigarettes in the hallway,
the flag on the pole thinks only
of the September sea.
On the last day of her life she notices
that her shoes are scuffed
but a dishy junior colleague
gives her a passing smile.

PAST ASHCOMBE

The curve past Ashcombe Church, my father's back
hunched tight above his bike, the sunlight hard
on both of us as silently we hoard
this hour against the weight of time's attack;

how many days of this have we got left?
The farms beneath us and the cooling wood
five sweating minutes on. This is our good
time: lost on narrow, snaking roads, the lift

of falcons rising sullen from their sleep,
two deer surprised beyond a crawling bend,
while sweat drops scald our eyes. Gone sixty and

the better cyclist, able still to keep
his lead, my father points a freckled hand
towards the wood, the moor, our journey's end.

PLUNDER

Only the pebbles and a meeting soon,
the wind from out the North, the surf backlashed
against itself, us two beside the smashed
breakwater holding little back, the moon

half-smothered by a rolling, oily cloud.
Two hundred years ago, the villagers
would wait for plunder from the razor spurs
of rock, ensnaring ships, the gale too loud

for any cry to carry. Now a sea,
empty of trade and threat alike, provides
no focus for the greedy. Finally

I knew we'd meet like this. Now who hides
their cruelty behind their nobler reasons?
We wait united by our separate treasons.

PROMOTION

Your rise has been remarkable and, yes,
you've worn your power with a lack of fuss,
taking the weight of others' deference
as if you barely noticed. Now we sense
a final shift to 'hard-won eminence'.

The term is grandiose but suitable;
there's something in you of a cardinal
eschewing pride and happy still to nod
among the younger priests, a fussy squad
who know your favour counts, your word is God.

What do I think of you? Some jealousy
but admiration too; I did not see
your quiet ambition – was it always there
or did our masters choose to give you air,
coaxing you onwards stair by giddy stair?

Well, this is you at forty-five: a Name,
the subtle player of a bruising game;
I miss the younger you. Why choose to prove
yourself like this, some itch for praise or love?
I hear your speech of thanks, then watch your
        workforce move.

RAPHAEL'S FRESCO

The great philosophers
are poised on the steps
of the School of Athens;

Socrates wears red,
Plato wears blue
and passion tempers reason.

It now seems doubtful
that I will ever visit
Raphael's fresco in Rome

but if things change
I'd like to believe
that I would go there often.

THE REST CURE

Easy enough to diagnose exhaustion,
you haven't had a holiday for years,
your luck is not as bad as it appears,
only your blunted mind's reiteration
exaggerates; a summer by the lake
will set you right, a long much-needed break.

Better to take a break before you break,
a sensible regime can curb exhaustion,
dive from the rock and let the cobalt lake
soak out the sorrow from the dismal years;
both love and guilt demand reiteration,
desert the city where her ghost appears.

Birches and ferns, sometimes a buck appears
poised in the shadow, waiting for the break
of the white spell to drive a reiteration
of hooves beyond the realm of your exhaustion;
learn from the deer and strip the awkward years
from off your back beside the waiting lake.

It's said a dead volcano holds this lake;
what if the tremor of the wind appears
snaking its way towards you from your years
of cockiness? You thought you could not break,
failing to see how stealthily exhaustion
whispers its tale, that cruel reiteration

of what we didn't do, the worse reiteration
of our stupidity. A tent, a lake,

a little mother-wit to curb exhaustion –
then guilt, formidable though it appears,
can be contained; so take this break
from who you've been for over thirty years.

Or would you rather roll the flood of years
back to their source, before reiteration
made guilt a habit that you dared not break?
A girl, a boy, a summer by the lake –
why make a myth of this? It just appears
ideal through time, through loss and through exhaustion.

Now by this lake you know no ghost appears
unless the years conspire with our exhaustion
though love may break us by reiteration.

RE-WATCHING FILMS

Re-watching films you feel
that given twenty years
your viewpoint slowly alters.

Take *Jaws*: I used to thrill
when three men fought their fears
and won on distant waters

but now I like the Mayor,
proud with the island's trust
to make the summer pay:

Ignore the shark – why scare
the tourists? Won't it just
get bored and swim away?

SPIDER

This gentle-fingered one
measures her path beyond
dipping branch and frond,
each trembling filament
may trigger her intent.

Gentle and gently gone,
I wish I had such courage
or could ignore her message:
when brinkmanship is best
the first leap is the test.

STRAY

'At first I thought she was a neighbour's cat
trying it on because they know I'm soft –
small thing she was with stripes. She knew my habits,
would come complaining as I left the house,
or when I fried myself a bit of bacon
she'd be there at the window looking tragic.

Of course I'd give her scraps, then gave her more,
soon I was buying treats and then I thought
"She's shy and won't come in but give her time ... "
Next thing there was that snow and someone knocked,
I didn't like to answer. Couple standing there,
nice couple I could tell: "Is that one yours?"

There in the blizzard was that blessèd cat
crouching beside my doorstep. So they took
her for themselves. Best thing for everyone.
I miss her though, daft thing, I miss her *need*
and more I miss responding to that need –
now isn't that silly?'

SURI

Suri likes the street mimes
with coins in each hand
we'll patrol the Embankment
numerous times
watching steampunk princesses
twirl their parasols,
gangsters make their final stand
and clockwork ballerinas
stutter into dance.

A bell-tower chimes
while a satyr seeks his lost
and long-dead love.
The gladiators
in their files
are all Spartacus.
Each improbable ghost
starts to move,
and Suri smiles.

THERE AND BACK

A night of travel, all your property
in five suitcases, drunk with lack of sleep
we reached the hotel, choosing first to creep
into the gaping bed. Eventually

we crossed six lanes of traffic and we saw
your college rooms, then sauntered slowly past
the town towards the Aran islands, a last
outpost of land beyond our rain-flecked shore.

Far off a tar-stained crane bent motionless,
'Nobody died,' you laughed, and you were right.
Trainbound, I watched the islands ebb away,

browsed through a Chekhov story, while the light
died down on Ireland's richness and the press
of tourists gathered in the drowsy passageway.

TIDAL LAW

Ten years of repetitious work had brought
me nothing, so with half a holiday
I trudged through seaweed, skipped a crumbling fort –
conjured by children in an hour of play –
and took towards the rocks. Fatigued in mind
I heard the waves discharge white shots of spray,
their twisting strands were hair-combed by the wind.
Two boats, named after girls, were tied before
an iron fence which gripped the cliff behind;
and by the ledge of dampened rock I saw
two greys: grey-green of sea, light grey of cloud,
a world illumined by a different law.
　I watched a figure ambling through the cold,
a ghosted self who never left this place
but took its loves and losses, growing old
without much hurry, at a gentle pace.
I tasted salt and heard a seabird call
and, turning, left the whiteness of that face
between the surging tide and the shrieking gull.

TODAY'S POST

The job rejection and my girlfriend sad,
consoling me. The interview went well,
I wish I knew ... and no I cannot tell
why someone else did better. When I've had
enough of pitying myself, we kiss,
she leaves for work (I have an evening shift).
Her scent still in the air, I stoop to lift
the blind and watch her run, already miss

her hand's cool touch. The family next door
heave round their punished car. The mother's shout
summons a final child. A drumbeat starts

across the street and on my pad I draw
a line, divide my life in equal parts:
the things I love / and those I would leave out.

TO A CRITIC WITH HIGH STANDARDS

Your style is doubtless elegant
but do you feel alive
still laying down the views at sixty
you held at twenty-five?

If *Hamlet* is too deep for us,
that's what re-reading's for;
change is the key but you my friend
have firmly locked the door.

TO MY WIFE

You watched as I became
a shambling skeleton
and took my gangling frame
on your small shoulder when
I could not stand upright,
then in my own despite
brought me to life again.

I know that gratitude
does not begin to pay
my debt. You raged and stood
by me through each cold day
waiting in hospitals
or making patient calls
while I wasted away

and most of all you fought
my half-expressed belief
that I should come to naught.
I thought of my last breath
withdrawing like sea foam;
stubborn, you saved me from
that waiting Winter death.

THE WEATHERMAN, 1944

Promptly at dawn the staff car waits,
the driver mumbling at the cold,
three men descend the chateau stairs
pulling their uniforms down straight,
surveying France in March: the dull
unhelpful plain, the earth torn bare.

Who would believe that war could be
so boring? Placidly, the men
watch from the car a waning moon;
the winter sun's ascendency
is minimal at best but then
the flare beneath the air balloon

centres their gaze. The car arrives,
my granddad rises in his basket,
watched by his comrades, fields retreat
like worries, something in him thrives
at such a height. He knows his task, it
surrounds him like a slow heartbeat.

There'll be no rain for six more days,
the enemy will make their push,
we have to mobilise or lose.
What Fate decided to raise
him sunwards where, in that brief hush,
he knew the coming weather and could use,

by some strange quirk of history
his gift of foresight for the Reich?

The staff car waits. I'd leave him poised
above the troops, the refugees
and games of feint and counterstrike,
still with his gods in the dawn's pulse.

WE STUDY KINDNESS

Ambitious of a certain fame
I wanted twenty years of work:
the time to make a modest name,
to win a minor kind of prize,
a steady burning of the wick.
The gods willed otherwise.

I'll meet my death in middle age,
no old man's fainting into night,
a sorting out of mortgages
and drugs before the last surprise,
much spitting but no noble fight;
the gods willed otherwise.

The worst is reaching fifty-one
and noticing how much I love
my stubborn wife. What can be done?
We study kindness; I devise
plans for us we'll never prove,
the gods will otherwise.

WEDDING RING

It seems a betrayal when I fail to wear you,
the comedy of wedlock states you must be
only removed for washing up and death;
frail silver compact, something we adhere to
in blindness, feeling step by step the gusty
high pathways where the timid lose their breath.

Some say you are an aphrodisiac:
'It's hot to steal a spouse – no strings attached!'
Should I regret I never found you so
or eased you off behind my sweating back
when parties turned risqué? Are we well-matched
in virtue or in fear – how would I know?

Perhaps all art is in the limitations
we set ourselves, so you encircle me
despite my doubts; I know 'I am that thing
they call a husband,' living on my rations
of long-term hopes and pleasures. We shall see
how this turns out – *where is my sodding ring?*

WINE TO WATER

The night is swollen with a taste like wine,
too full, too close, and through the plastered wall
the voices start, insistent, slow, a fine

trickle of wrongs, the tepid rain of all
the gentleness our loves cannot provide.
A rumbling reply, dull at first, too full

of long work days for righteousness or pride
but this will change. Each vented word draws blood,
I twist beneath my quilt as if to hide;

no good. I watch a square of cloud. They flood
our concrete flats with sudden storms of loss,
the fear of never being understood

stains through the dowdy walls and seeps across
each lighted stairway. Neighbours make no fuss,
next time the shouting starts it might be us.

A DIFFERENT PREY

An autumn day
in Italy:
walking the ornamental gardens
past ponds of carp
towards the hills
and the inevitable fountain

where Actaeon
sees Diana
naked and bathing with her nymphs,
so he is turned
into a deer
and eaten by his hunting dogs;

I liked the statue
and even more
the fountain water on my skin;
but now I question
what stony gaze
ordained my slower transformation?

My limbs are thin
as any deer's
turning its last and puzzled look
towards the grove;
with changing senses
I hear the barking of the hounds.

ANNE

I met a very nice transsexual nurse
who took me for a fellow Londoner:
Nothing surprises us, we've seen it all…

Over biscuits, restored to consciousness,
the specialist confirmed my cancer tumour;
loyal to Anne, I tried to look unfussed:

we Londoners have really seen it all.

FEEDING CROWS
(A voice heard during radiotherapy)

Disliking poems inspired by dreams
today I am inflicted by one:
a crisp and sexless voice declares
'Go feed the crows ... or feed the crows!'
and tells me words to speak out loud.
These steroids fill my mind with crap.

Not three hours later, on the beach,
baguette in hand I circle bread
before the hunched, suspicious crows,
then murmur at the rain-specked sea:
Apollo, king of crows, save me.

GOAT SONG

What better than those gentle afternoons,
learning a lover's most important lesson?
Patient to tease, to lap, to stop or press on,
caught in the urgency of *now* or *soon*...

until I rode your tide, still kissing as
your heel cupped round my skull or pushed me back
and so we'd rest before love's next attack,
a blameless way to let a summer pass.

Back then I was an ignorant young goat
learning to find my joy in pleasing you;
twenty years on, it's curious to note
our pastimes may have caused my cancered throat:
a nobler cause than cigarettes, it's true,
but quite a footnote on the verb 'to screw'.

IN THE NIGHT WARD

So what are you in for?
I'm barely through the door
but Ray has little time
for niceties, turns out
his cancer's worse than mine.

Six foot and now six stone,
his hourly night-long groan
quivers like a soft chime
'oh God...' until no doubt
he's rationed more morphine.

He claims that seventy-two
is young to die. It's true
enough. I nod and climb
into my bed. Lights out,
I tell myself I'm fine.

JUST BREATHE

The mask is lowered on my face
then screwed down to the table, tight.
Just breathe: good, sensible advice
except two times this week my fight
for air has made the process stop;
just breathe: I'm not here on this altar,
I am in bed, my cat on top,
the mask a stray sheet, do not falter.

Just breathe and gaze towards a poster
of Spring, her back towards me, hand
brushing a bud, she walks no faster
than three miles an hour, understand
that step of life. Beneath my mask
I pray to join her – too much to ask?

NAUSEA AND THE DIGNITY OF SUFFERING

So this is me,
thinner and much balder
and rather sick
from yesterday's attack:

the dignity
of suffering? I wonder,
something sticks
in me at such a cheap crack.

Better to be
a magpie in winter
picking the ticks
off a sheep's back.

NINE WAYS OF LOOKING
AT A CHEMOTHERAPY WARD
'I am glad to the brink of fear.' R.W. Emerson

1
As I am plugged in
to the drip-feed
a single magpie
peers over the gutter.

2
The nurses are jubilant:
payday tomorrow!

3
'Patients are very
territorial;
some even have lucky
chair numbers.'

4
The four mosaics
in the hospital garden
figure the four seasons.

I like the cobalt sky
and snowflakes of winter.

5
After an hour
another patient arrives:
'Morning, trouble!'

He plays a drum-roll
on his armchair rests.

6
Is anything more calming
than early autumn
sunlight on a stack
of hospital pillows
warming by the window?

7
The sunlight
caresses my arm
and the woman opposite
removes her wig.

8
On her visit,
the dietician
(who is leaving next week)
notes the growing looseness
of my wedding ring.

9
I have watched the garden
for ten hours
and not one bird
has landed.

I see only
the reflection of seagulls
gliding past
the windows of other wards.

PHOTO BEFORE CHEMO

My hand rests on a lion's back
(marble of course) in Italy,
the stairwell of some Bourbon palace;

I clearly swelter: convex belly
stuck to my shirt, my face near puce,
my grin remoulds my double-chin.

Today I have a different look,
I haven't been this slim since twenty
with killer cheekbones, my arms so thin

you might well think me underfed,
topped by a lean and mean shaved head.
My hand rests on a lion's back.

SCALP

On that last Friday
I was made of crystal
and transparent to
sunlight and sea-glare;

my hair especially
was like shards, somehow
detachable. Why be
surprised when they broke free,

coming out in clumps
in my post-walk shower,
handfuls to be gathered
and quickly binned?

Later as the barber
shaved my wisps away
I saw the new me
with sudden recognition:

not bad, I thought, not bad,
crystal this morning,
bare rock this afternoon
and all in under four hours.

INVASION OF THE BODY SNATCHER

Odd how these crazes now come back:
like Science Fiction, watching as
the stealthy aliens attack
with duplicates designed to pass
as us: sleepwalkers, slowly paced,
doubles for victims they've replaced.
Not that farfetched as it transpires
my medicines have changed my smell,
my thoughts and even my desires.
My old friends ask me if I'm well
and faithfully refuse to drop me
but watch with puzzlement and fear
this me: the slow, diminished copy
of someone previously here.

THE SWIMMER

Beyond the lighthouse, past the ramparts,
my belly tight with air, I let
my buoyancy expunge my past;
I've heard I have a 'swimmer's ears':
something to do with years of pressure
remoulding their grooves and contours –
a doctor's joking observation
before a different immersion.
The town surrounds the sleeping hill,
a shop for ice cream and the chill
of autumn, while a gliding gull
checks me out. Many men lose weight,
others long for a slimmer waist,
why fret about some test results?
Beyond the lighthouse and the deckchairs,
the water cools my swimmer's ears.

Sean Elliott: A Personal Appreciation

'Theatre Usher', a poem from his London sequence, was inspired by Sean Elliott's own time working at the National Theatre. In this the Usher is both the most marginal participant in a performance of Hamlet, and is placed centre stage. Hamlet too was both actor and audience, and the unlikely kinship discovered here, both ominous and unexpected, between the Prince and the attendant, allows for a new and enlightening perspective. Standing outside the auditorium, experiencing that sense of shared isolation peculiar to great cities, and waiting as the tragic hero must, the Usher commands a vast nocturnal panorama: 'I nurse my patience, curb a sense of loss/that comes more often now, and stand unseen//but happy...'

As both hero and functionary, the Usher inhabits so many contradictions that his status might rightly be compared to that of Schrödinger's cat, that theoretical creature who is, at the same time, both alive and dead.

Shakespeare figures also in the title poem, included here, of Sean's first collection, 'Waterhouse and the Tempest'. Here the Victorian artist, already dying, and having out-lived his age, is excluded from his own painted vision of the magic isle, yet, in another unexpected connection, he touches Shakespeare's world through the ability to imagine, as Miranda does, the suffering of others.

I first met Sean when he was teaching Shakespeare at London University. He was, I think, an enviably good teacher because he was himself creative. Over lunches in Deptford, or off the Charing Cross Road, I soon had some sense of the range of his fertile literary curiosity, as he explained an admiration for Schopenhauer, discussed obscure theatrical productions or French cinema, or the book he had written on Restoration Drama.

Further evidence was the extraordinary working library that filled his home, like the stacks of an unconventional institution, watched over by his own very real cats. One of these appearing in another poem, was, it seems, tamed by having read to him Poe's 'Annabel Lee' (another maiden who, like Miranda, dwelt on the margin between sea and land). The cat, who may or may not understand the poem within a poem, listens contentedly to Poe's tales that describe an anomalous state poised between life and death, a state enjoyed here also by the dream-phantom of Poe himself.

Sean's poetry though is not that of alienation or uncertainty, or of being relegated to a half-life. He possessed what might be called an observational sensibility. Self-aware and able to express itself with great clarity, it enjoys a position outside, from which it is able to discover un-thought-of connections, connections which show that it has, in some unexpected way, been on the inside all along.

His poems let us see that those who appear to, or as Sean was forced to do by illness, retreat into a cave of books can be those who are most involved in the world, and remind us that those who lose their voices and are no longer here to chat with us, can now speak to us most clearly.

Simon Reynolds, 2019

For Sean

Sitting in the kitchen beside me at my feet, Shelley and Fritz prick up their ears, imagining they hear their Master's voice which has now become an echo. But his voice lives in this collection, which will allow those readers who have known him to meet him once more through his poems – and allow those who haven't met him to get to know him for the first time.

Like Sean, the cats and myself have been on a journey together, investigating our past, present and future. Sean's journey was never one of loneliness, and he has not travelled into oblivion – but into a place to be remembered for the singularity of his soul and his spirit.

The sea always played an important part in our lives. Sean grew up by the sea, I came to England via the sea where I met him in a sea of thoughts, and we lived by the sea for the rest of his life. The cats and I left again by the sea in 2016, this time without Sean. I took a load of books with me, his books, which have been his surroundings, his cavern, his beacon and his fortress from early on in his life. They have also been the first link between us in our conversations, our shared thoughts, our outlook on life and humanity. And they are abundant – just as his poetry has been …

Sean was multi-faceted and despite being very shy and self-deprecating was a very funny man. He was capable of displaying an immensely dark sense of humour if you had the privilege of knowing him, of sharing with him his motives and views ... and in my case his life.

'We Study Kindness' was the last poem he wrote, five days before his death. It was translated into German and then incorporated into the eulogy read at his funeral which took place at a location he had chosen long before he had fallen ill. This was one of his last wishes – in addition to his desire that one last book of his would be published posthumously, That has now been granted.

May our life together stay private as it is, as it was – suffice to say that it was a journey through love, thrill, joy, illusion and fun, frustration, sweetness, anger, overcoming, despair and hope ... and yet, in the end, defeat by the indomitable Master of Us All.

Jules Elliott-Riley, 2019

Sean Elliott: Magazine Publication

'Photo from Before', *The Rialto* 85 (2016): 45.

'The Magician's Wife', *Acumen* 81 (2015): 30.

'Omens', *Tears in the Fence* 57(2013): 49.

'Bad Script, Good Film', *The Rialto* 75 (2013): 22.

'On Running Out of Money', *Other Poetry* 4th Ser 5 (2012): 44.

'Staying True', *The Reader* 45 (2012): 40.

'Double Act', *The Interpreter's House* 49 (2012): 22.

'Dead Crabs', *The Interpreter's House* 47 (2011): 28.

'Reassuring News', *The Rialto* 72 (2011): 25.

'Edgar and Sam', *Weyfarers* 109 (2010): 5.

'Examinations', *Weyfarers* 109 (2010): 13.

'Good Advice', *Acumen* 68 (2010): 87.

'Reading King Lear', *Magma* 47 (2010): 82.

'Advancement', *The Rialto* 68 (2010): 36.

'The Status of the Cat', *The Interpreter's House* 42 (2009): 24.

'Domestic Behaviour', *Poetry Review* 99.2 (2009): 31.

'Our Ghosts', *South* 39 (2009): 34 and *Weyfarers* 106 (2009): 30.

'Margate', *The Liberal* Spring 2009: 15.

'Pat', *Other Poetry* 3rd Ser 3 (2008): 41.

'Grossmütter', *Penniless Press* 26 (2008): 43.

'In Defence of Realism', *Dream Catcher* 22 (2008): 127

'Dead Stock', *Iota* 82 (2008): 43.

'Kent', *London Magazine* June/July 2008: 43.

'Commuting on Christmas Eve', *Acumen* 61 (May 2008): 71.

'Bangladesh 1977', *The Reader* 27 (2007): 59.

'Background Radio', *The Reader* 27 (2007): 59.

'This Actor's Laughter', *The Liberal* Apr/May 2007: 21.

'Local Wines', *The Rialto* 61 (Winter 2006): 46.

'The Octopus', *Other Poetry* 2nd Ser 31 (2006): 18.

'Saloons and Tomahawks', *The Interpreter's House* 33 (2006): 27.

'The Escape', *Iota* 75 (2006): 23.

'Well Spoken', *Penniless Press* 23 (Summer 2006): 14.

'More Soldiers', *Smiths Knoll* 38 (2006): 45.

'There and Back', *Obsessed with Pipework* 34 (2006): 10.

'Film-maker', *Iota* 72 (2005): 46.

'Birthday Party', *The Interpreter's House* 30 (2005): 24.

'The Football Stand', *The Interpreter's House* 30 (2005): 25.

'Butchery', *Other Poetry* 2nd Ser 28 (2005): 28.

'Not Too Badly', *London Magazine* Aug/Sept 2005: 17.

'Night Song', *Seam* 23 (2005):23.

'Threesome', *Seam* 23 (2005): 24.

'Plunder', *The Liberal* July/Aug 2005: 29.

'Wine to Water', *The Reader* 18 (2005): 76.

'More Statues Please', *Acumen* 52 (May 2005): 54.

'In the Café', *The Rialto* 57 (2005): 30.

'Home Through Camden', *Tears in the Fence* 40 (2005): 66.

'Ajax', *The Interpreter's House* 28 (2005): 23.

'The Golem', *Staple* 61 (Winter 2004): 22.

'First Days', *Iota* 68 (2004): 4.

'Past Ashcombe', *Other Poetry* 2nd Ser 26 (2004): 23.

'Her Grandparents', *Other Poetry* 2nd Ser 26 (2004): 24.

'Today's Post', *Seam* 21 (2004): 17.

'Wedding Day', *Seam* (2004): 18.

'Child Minding', *The Reader* 15 (2004):53.

'Making Sense', *The Reader* 15 (2004): 53.

'Giraffe', *Acumen* 48 (Jan 2004): 36.

'Long Distance' *Agenda* 39.4 (2003): 274

'Mother Kindness', *Agenda* 39.4 (2003): 275.

'From the Chapel', *Agenda* 39.4 (2003): 275.

'Malediction on Critical Theory', *Other Poetry* 2nd Ser 24 (2003): 30.

'Outclassed', *Seam* 19 (2003): 32.

'Jenkintown. PA', *Seam* 19 (2003): 33.

'The Waiting Room', *Iota* 61 (2003): 51.

'The Farm', *Other Poetry* 2nd Ser 22 (2003): 39.

'Again', *Other Poetry* 2nd Ser 22 (2003): 40.

'Mezzo Cammin', *Thumbscrew* 20-21 (2002): 25.

'Home in March', *Tears in the Fence* 32 (2002): 68.

'Three Brothers', *The Rialto* 51 (2002): 9.

'Theatre Usher', *Other Poetry* 2nd Ser 20 (2002): 34.

'His Swans', *The Interpreter's House* 18 (2001): 20.

'The Migration', *Smiths Knoll* 26 (2001): 20.

'Winter Tourists', *Smiths Knoll* 26 (2001): 55.

'Cloakroom Attendant', *Poetry Review* 91.3 (2001): 85-86.

'The Boat Ride', *Poetry Review* 91.3 (2001): 86-87.

'Back to Dawlish', *Tears in the Fence* 29 (2001): 69.

'Indira's Laundry', *Seam* 15 (2001): 41.

'Dawlish in April', *Seam* 15 (2001): 42.

'Cassandra', *The Interpreter's House* 17 (2001): 12.

'In Memory of Peter Levi', *Other Poetry* 2nd Ser 18 (2001): 46.

'New Cross', *Other Poetry* 2nd Ser 17 (2000): 40.

'Waterhouse and the Tempest', *Connections* 22 (2000): 6.

'Lea Mount', *PN Review* Jan-Feb 2000: 17.

'The Woods', *PN Review* Jan-Feb 2000: 17.

'Fidelity', *PN Review* Jan-Feb 2000: 17.

'Tidal Law', *Agenda* 37.1 (1999): 47.

'Morning on the Coast', *Agenda* 37.1 (1999): 48.

'Otherwise', *London Magazine* Oct-Nov 1998: 21.

'A Christmas Visit', *Seam* 10 (1998): 70-71.